Before the Seed

How Pollen Moves

Susannah Buhrman-Deever

illustrated by

Gina Triplett & Matt Curtius

≡ mit Kids Press

We live in a world of green, of fields and forests
filled with plants that grow . . .

from seeds.

But before the seeds grow the green . . .

pollen needs to move.

But pollen is tiny, each grain no bigger than a speck of dust.

✻ Pollen is made by flowers, on a part called the stamen. A flower begins making seeds when pollen lands on a different part of the flower, called the stigma. This movement of pollen, from stamen to stigma, is called pollination.

It has no wings, no wheels, and no feet. How can pollen move?

Plants have found ways.

✻ Sometimes, pollen from the same flower can make a seed. But most of the time, pollen has farther to go: to another flower on the same plant or another of the same kind of plant. No matter how far it moves, pollen can only make a seed when it meets up with the same kind of plant it came from.

Some plants have flowers that launch their pollen onto a puff of air, to be scattered far and wide by the wind.

✳ There are at least 25,000 different kinds of wind-pollinated plants. Pollen grains from these plants are dry and light, so the wind can carry them farther. To have a chance of hitting their targets, wind-pollinated plants have to release a lot of pollen. A single birch flower can release 5.5 million pollen grains. A whole tree, billions.

✳ Tape grass (*Vallisneria*) is a water plant with male flowers that make pollen and female flowers where seeds grow. The male flowers start out underwater. The female flowers bloom at the surface. When the time is right, the plant releases the male flowers, and they rise up to the surface. There, the male flower's petals curve open, helping it float along like a boat. When the male flower reaches a surface-floating female flower, it falls into the female flower and pollinates it.

Others have flowers that set sail across the water,
hoping their pollen will land in just the right place.

But most flowering plants, over three hundred thousand
kinds, don't do this most important of jobs alone.

Their pollen is carried on the bodies of beetles and bees.

✳ There are at least 20,000 different species of bees in the world, with approximately 4,000 different species from North America alone. Some species visit many kinds of flowers. Other species visit just a few.

✳ Beetles are the oldest known pollinator (an animal that carries pollen). Scientists have found 99-million-year-old fossilized beetles covered with pollen. Today, 77,000 beetle species visit flowers.

It is dusted onto fur and feathers,

✴ Bats are the main pollinator for more than 500 different kinds of plants. Each bat visits hundreds of flowers a night, and they are especially good at carrying pollen among plants that are spread far apart because they can fly long distances.

✴ Around 2,000 different bird species pollinate flowers, including hummingbirds, sunbirds, and honeyeaters. Unlike insects that don't fly in the rain, birds can travel between flowers in all kinds of weather.

or clings to mouths and wings, tongues and toes.

✳ Most butterflies and moths carry pollen on their proboscises (flexible straw-like tongues), mouths, legs, and heads. The eastern tiger swallowtail (*Papilio glaucus*) carries the pollen of the flame azalea (*Rhododendron calendulaceum*) on its wings, dusting the flowers with pollen as it flaps.

✳ Flies pollinate at least 555 species of plants around the world, including many foods we eat, like tea and onions. Flies are the main pollinators in the Arctic, where the freezing temperatures and strong winds make it hard for many other insect pollinators, like most bees, to survive.

Before the seeds grow the green, animals
move pollen from flower to flower.

How do the animals find
the flowers?

✳ Clumps of pollen from an African grassland
orchid (*Disa chrysostachya*) stick to the toes of
the malachite sunbird (*Nectarinia famosa*) when
it perches on the orchid's tall flower stalks.

Plants show them where to go using color and scent and even sound.

✳ The colors of flowers help them stand out and often match the colors their pollinators can see best.

✳ The scent of honeysuckle (*Lonicera periclymenum*) guides the elephant hawk-moth (*Deilephila elpenor*) to the flowers at night. Honey bees remember the scents of flowers they've visited and fly toward them if they smell the scent again.

✳ Many bats use echolocation to navigate in the dark. The *Marcgravia evenia* vine has special dish-shaped leaves above its flowers. The shape of these leaves helps bounce back a bat's sounds, so the bat can easily find the flowers.

✳ Female blow flies (Calliphoridae) lay their eggs on dead animals. After the eggs hatch, the blow fly larvae eat the rotting body. Carrion flowers (*Stapelia gigantea*) mimic dead animals. The flowers have dark red centers and smell rotten. The blow flies land on carrion flowers to lay their eggs, pollinating the flowers in the process. But their larvae will starve, since there will be no meat to eat after they hatch.

Before the seeds grow the green, plants invite their pollinators to visit. But why do the animals come?

Sometimes they come because plants play tricks, pretending to be something they're not.

✳ The broad-lipped bird orchid (*Chiloglottis trapeziformis*) smells just like a female thynnine wasp (*Neozeleboria cryptoides*). Male wasps visit the flowers, thinking they have found a mate, but end up carrying the orchid's pollen instead.

But most of the time . . .

the animals come because the plants offer them a reward. Sweet sips of nectar and extra protein-packed pollen to eat.

※ Nectar (a sugary liquid made in a flower's nectary) is an important part of the diet of many pollinators, giving them a boost of energy.

※ Bees feed their larvae with pollen. The pollen from bat-pollinated flowers has extra protein to better nourish their larger bodies.

※ *Clusia odorata* flowers make resins that are collected by stingless bees *Trigona pallens*. The bees use them to build waterproof nests.

* Male orchid bees (Euglossini) collect scented oils from orchids, which they pack into pouches on their legs. They use the scent to attract mates.

And sometimes sticky, gluey resins or perfumed oils. Or even a cozy place to keep warm.

* Arum lilies (*Philodendron solimoesense*) heat up during the night. This heat helps the scarab beetles (*Cyclocephala colasi*) that pollinate them keep warm, enabling them to save energy.

We live in a world of green, with fields and forests full of plants that grow from seeds. Before the seeds grow the green, most flowering plants and their pollinators help each other.

But a plant's rewards for its pollinators do not come free. Plants use energy to make pollen and nectar, resins and oils and heat. How can a plant make sure that its rewards don't go to waste?

Some flowers have shapes that help their pollen hit its target. They may have tubes built for hummingbird bills, with parts that bend to bless their crowns . . .

* As an Anna's hummingbird (*Calypte anna*) beats its wings, it builds up a charge of static electricity around its body. When it approaches a tree tobacco flower (*Nicotiana glauca*), the electric charge bends the stamens toward the hummingbird's head and helps stick the pollen to it.

or a fit made for the face of a mosquito,
so the flower can gently, gently kiss its
eyes with pollen.

✳ The blunt-veined orchid
(*Platanthera obtusata*) is
pollinated by the snow pool
mosquito (*Aedes communis*). As
the mosquito slips its head into the
flower to drink the nectar, a cluster
of pollen is glued to the mosquito's
eyes. When the mosquito drinks
from the next flower, the pollen on
the mosquito's eyes stick to that
flower's stigma.

Others may let only their preferred partners retrieve their rewards.

Some hold tight to their pollen. It can only be loosened by the buzziest of bees.

Some can only be opened by strong hands.

✳ Tomatoes don't let their pollen fall on just any visitor, but bumble bees can shake it loose. When they visit tomato flowers, they grab on and vibrate their bodies at just the right rate to shower their bodies with pollen.

✳ The flowers of the traveler's tree (*Ravenala madagascariensis*) are sealed tight with stiff coverings. Black lemurs (*Eulemur macaco*) use their strong hands to pull the coverings apart before burying their faces inside to drink the nectar.

While others have passages so narrow that only a tiny fly the size of a poppy seed can slip inside, coating its body with pollen like a sprinkling of sugar.

✳ Tiny biting midges (Ceratopogonidae) might be only 1 millimeter long, but they have a big job. They are the only known pollinator of cacao trees (*Theobroma cacao*), whose seeds we use to make chocolate.

And some hide their nectar down tubes so deep, it can only be reached by tongues that are impossibly long.

✻ Long-proboscid flies (*Moegistorhynchus longirostris*) are key pollinators of at least twenty different flower species on South Africa's west coast. The flowers it pollinates have long tubes of 1 ¼ – 2 ¾ inches (32–71 millimeters). The fly has a long proboscis to match, up to eight times the length of its body.

 * The partnership between yucca moths and
yucca plants has lasted at least 40 million years. Only
yucca moths pollinate yucca plants, and the moths'
entire life cycle depends on the yucca. The
moths emerge from underground cocoons in
spring as the yucca blooms. After the moths
mate on the blossoms, the female moth
gathers pollen in special tentacles around
her mouth. Then she carries the pollen to
a different yucca flower and pollinates it.
Finally, she lays her eggs inside the flower,
where the seeds will develop. After her eggs
hatch, the moth larvae eat the yucca seeds. But
enough seeds are left uneaten to become new yucca
plants.

And some plants and pollinators are so dependent on each other, so perfectly connected, that neither could exist without the other . . .

because pollen needs to move before the seeds . . .

grow the world of green.

MORE ABOUT FLOWERS

Flowers come in all shapes, sizes, and colors, depending on how they are pollinated.

Although there is no "typical" flower, they usually have these parts:

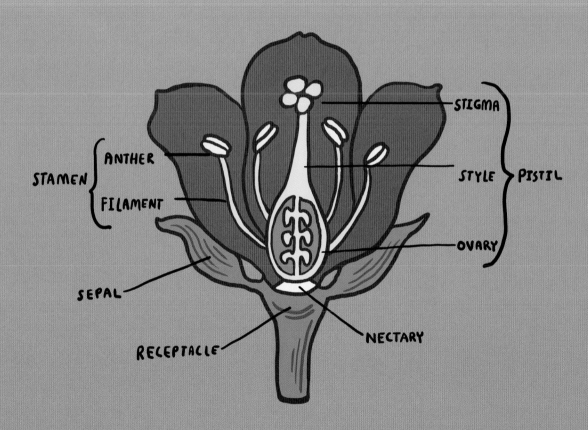

PISTIL: The female part of the flower. Each pistil holds one or more ovaries, a style, and a stigma.

STIGMA: Where pollen grains attach and germinate.

STYLE: Connects the stigma and the ovary.

OVARY: Where the ovules (tiny eggs) are made, and where the seeds develop after pollination.

STAMEN: The male part of the flower. It contains the anther and the filament.

ANTHER: The part of the stamen where pollen is made.

FILAMENT: A stalk that holds the anther up.

SEPAL: The outermost part of the flower. It covers the other flower parts when in bud.

PETAL: The colored part of the flower.

NECTARY: Makes nectar for pollinators. (Not all flowers have nectaries. These flowers may offer other rewards, like extra pollen or scented oils, for their pollinators.)

SOME PLANT SPECIES have both male and female parts in the same flower. Others have two types of flowers: one male form (with the pollen-producing parts) and a female one (with the seed-producing parts). In some species, these two types of flowers can be found on the same plant. In other species, only one type of flower can be found per plant.

POLLINATORS IN PERIL

Plants and the animals that pollinate them have relationships that evolved over millions and millions of years. Pollinators help plants make seeds. They also help us. More than 75 percent of all plants people eat are pollinated by animals. The more types of pollinators around, the better. Farmers can increase the amount of crops they can grow in the same amount of space if more kinds of insects visit their plants.

But pollinators are at risk. In the last fifty years, honey bee numbers have fallen by half in the United States. And honey bees are not the only ones in trouble. In some areas of the United States, half of native bee species have disappeared from where they once lived.

What's causing this decline? Pesticides can kill pollinators even if those pollinators don't nest in fields where they are sprayed. Climate change is also putting pressure on pollinators. Bumble bees have suffered from an increase in extreme heat events. As weather patterns change, the timing of flowering and insect life cycles may go out of sync. This could be especially challenging for those pollinators that depend on just a few plant species. Habitat loss is another major cause. As people develop more and more land, a smaller variety of plants and fewer nesting sites are available for insects, birds, and bats.

BUT THERE ARE WAYS YOU CAN HELP. HERE'S HOW:

✳ If you have a yard or share a community garden, ask your parents, family, and community not to use pesticides.

✳ Leave your garden "messy." Old plant stems can make good nest sites for native leaf-cutting bees and mason bees. Keep bare patches of earth for native ground-nesting bumble bees to nest in. And piles of old logs and leaves provide shelter from heat.

✳ Grow host plants for butterflies and moths. Different species need different plants for their larvae to feed on.

✳ Grow plants that are native to your area, especially ones that bloom in early spring, to help early-spring native bees.

✳ Grow a variety of different plants that bloom at different times to provide food all year round.

FOR MORE INFORMATION ON POLLINATION AND POLLINATORS:

BOOKS

Levine, Sara. *Flower Talk: How Plants Use Color to Communicate*. Minneapolis, MN: Millbrook Press, 2019.

Pattison, Darcy. *Pollen: Darwin's 130 Year Prediction*. Little Rock, AR: Mims House, 2019.

Slade, Suzanne. *What If There Were No Bees? A Book About the Grassland Ecosystem*. Mankato, MN: Picture Window Books, 2011.

WEBSITES

Pollinator Partnership: www.pollinator.org

US Forest Service: www.fs.usda.gov/managing-land/wildflowers/pollinators

Xerces Society for Invertebrate Conservation: www.xerces.org

SELECTED BIBLIOGRAPHY

Bao, Tong, Bo Wang, Jianguo Li, and David Dilcher. "Pollination of Cretaceous Flowers." *Proceedings of the National Academy of Sciences* 116, no. 49 (December 3, 2019): 24707–24711.

Cox, Paul Alan. "Water-pollinated Plants." *Scientific American* 269, no. 4 (October 1993): 68–74.

McAlister, Erica. *The Secret Life of Flies*. Buffalo, NY: Firefly Books, 2017.

Pauw, Anaton, Jaco Stofberg, and Richard J. Waterman. "Flies and Flowers in Darwin's Race." *Evolution* 63, no. 1 (January 14, 2009): 268–279.

Pellmyr, Olle, and James Leebens-Mack. "Forty Million Years of Mutualism: Evidence for Eocene Origin of the Yucca-Yucca Moth Association." *Proceedings of the National Academy of Sciences* 96 (August 3, 1999): 9178–9183.

Potts, Simon G., Jacobus C. Biesmeijer, Claire Kremen, Peter Neumann, Oliver Schweiger, and William E. Kundin. "Global Pollinator Declines: Trends, Impacts and Drivers." *Trends in Ecology and Evolution* 25, no. 6 (June 2010): 345–353.

Proctor, Michael, Peter Yeo, and Andrew Lack. *The Natural History of Pollination*. Portland, OR: Timber Press, 1996.

Seymour, Roger S., Craig R. White, and Marc Gibernau. "Environmental Biology: Heat Reward for Insect Pollinators." *Nature* 426 (November 20, 2003): 243–244.

Simon, Ralph, Marc W. Holderied, Corinna U. Koch, and Otto von Helversen. "Floral Acoustics: Conspicuous Echoes of a Dish-Shaped Leaf Attract Bat Pollinators." *Science* 333 (July 29, 2011): 631–633.

SUSANNAH BUHRMAN-DEEVER has a PhD in behavioral biology, specializing in animal behavior and ecology. She is the author of *Predator and Prey*, illustrated by Bert Kitchen, and *If You Take Away the Otter*, illustrated by Matthew Trueman. Susannah Buhrman-Deever lives with her husband and sons in New York State, where she enjoys hiking through forests, paddling on the water, and puttering in her garden.

GINA TRIPLETT and **MATT CURTIUS** are a wife-and-husband artistic team who have projects ranging from public art to advertising to print books for children and adults. Individually, Gina Triplett has exhibited her art throughout the United States and abroad, and Matt Curtius is an associate professor at University of the Arts in Philadelphia.

Text copyright © 2024 by Susannah Buhrman-Deever
Illustrations copyright © 2024 by Gina and Matt LLC

First edition 2024

Library of Congress Catalog Card Number pending
ISBN 978-1-5362-2657-7

23 24 25 26 27 28 APS 10 9 8 7 6 5 4 3 2 1

Printed in Humen, Dongguan, China

This book was typeset in Filosofia and Gilroy.
The illustrations were created digitally, incorporating scans of ink and acrylic paint.

MIT Kids Press
an imprint of Candlewick Press
99 Dover Street
Somerville, Massachusetts 02144

mitkidspress.com
candlewick.com